CLARINET in A
(alternative to Cor Anglais)

O Lord, thou hast searched me out

JOHN RUTTER

(TIME TO TURN)

This instrumental part accompanies the vocal score of the anthem (X476).

OXFORD UNIVERSITY PRESS MUSIC DEPARTMENT, GREAT CLARENDON STREET, OXFORD OX2 6DP
The Moral Rights of the Composer have been asserted. Photocopying this copyright material is ILLEGAL.

Cl. in A

Cl. in A

Spi – rit:___ or whi–ther shall I go then from thy pre – sence?

If I climb up in – to hea – ven,___ thou art there:_____ If I

go down to hell,_____ thou art there al–so._____ If I

take the wings of the morn – ing:___ and re – main___ in the ut – ter–most parts of the sea;

77 Ev - en there shall thy hand lead me: and thy right hand shall hold me.

81 **F** mf risoluto f mf

85 If I say, Per-ad-ven-ture the dark-ness shall cov-er me: then shall my mp mf mp

90 **G** night be turned to day. Yea, the dark-ness is no mf p

(TIME TO TURN)

Cl. in A

dark - ness with thee, ____ but the night is as clear as the day:

mp

the dark-ness and light to thee are both a - like.____

f *mp*

poco rit.

I will give thanks un-to thee, for I am fear - ful-ly and won-der-ful-ly made:

a tempo   **accel.**   **(accel.)**

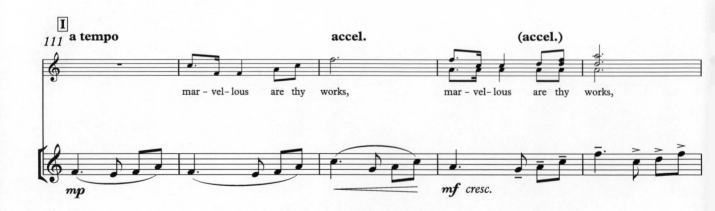

mar - vel-lous are thy works,   mar - vel-lous are thy works,

mp   *mf cresc.*

Cl. in A

Con moto maestoso ♩ = 80

mar – vel – lous,____ mar – vel – lous,____ mar – vel – lous.____

poco rallentando

A tempo, meno mosso ♩ = 66

Try me, O God, and seek the ground of my heart:____ prove me, and ex –

rallentando

J Tempo I (Lento) ♩ = 56

– a – mine my thoughts.____ O

Lord,____ thou hast searched me out, and known me.____

rit.

dim.

ISBN 978-0-19-335980-2

www.oup.com

9 780193 359802